GENETIC DISEASES AND GENE THERAPIES

AUTISM

Richard Spilsbury

rosen publishing's
**rosen
central**

New York

Published in 2019 by The Rosen Publishing Group, Inc.
29 East 21st Street
New York, NY 10010

Produced for Rosen by Calcium Creative Ltd
Editors for Calcium: Sarah Eason and Kris Hirschmann
Designer: Simon Borrough
Picture researcher: Rachel Blount

Photo credits: Cover: Shutterstock: Amiak: bottom right; Andrii Muzyka: bottom; PT Images: main; Inside: Shutterstock: Asia Images Group: p. 20; Samuel Borges Photography: p. 29; Valery Brozhinsky: p. 41; Ozgur Coskun: p. 17; Creatista: p. 31; Early Spring: p. 27; ESB Professional: p. 32; Goldquest: p. 35; GraphicMama: p. 30; Humpback_Whale: p. 15; Denis Kuvaev: p. 19; Monkey Business Images: p. 22; Moopixel: p. 13; Neirfy: p. 34; Nobeastsofierce: p. 37; Numstocker: p. 14; Pavla: pp. 24, 47; Photocreo Michal Bednarek: p. 21; Photographee.eu: pp. 7, 26; Ra2studio: p. 4; Rawpixel.com: p. 5; Rost9: p. 18; Science Photo: p. 39; Syr_y: p. 38; TonyV3112: p. 8; Yakobchuk Vasyl: p. 10; Meletios Verras: p. 12; Andrii Vodolazhskyi: p. 11; Steven Wright: p. 44; Wikimedia Commons: Lance Cpl. Andrea Ovalle: p. 43b; Rama: p. 40; Ferdinand Schmutzer: p. 43t.

Cataloging-in-Publication Data

Names: Spilsbury, Richard.
Title: Autism / Richard Spilsbury.
Description: New York : Rosen Central, 2019. | Series: Genetic diseases and gene therapies | Includes glossary and index.
Identifiers: LCCN ISBN 9781508182665 (pbk.) | ISBN 9781508182658 (library bound)
Subjects: LCSH: Autism in children—Juvenile literature. | Autistic children—Juvenile literature.
Classification: LCC RJ506.A9 S646 2019 | DDC 618.92'85882—dc23

Manufactured in the United States of America

Contents

Chapter 1

What Is Autism?

At a party, you might have to move closer to hear the person you are speaking to. You cannot hear well over the background noises of music, talking, eating, and laughter. For some people, the noises of such a party are overwhelming. They hear absolutely everything at the same volume. This could be a fork touching someone's teeth, the sound of someone brushing his or her hair, or distant talking and laughter. Other people might view the world differently. For example, they might literally feel what they see. Or, they might experience a casual touch as a burning sensation or an electric shock. People who sense the world in ways like this may have a condition called autism.

People with autism experience and react to the world differently than those without the condition.

Processing Differences

Autism is a neurodevelopmental disorder. This means it is an impairment of the development and growth of the brain and nervous system. As a result, people with autism process information differently than most people. They also experience the world and people around them differently. Everyone with autism has some form of sensory struggle with sight, sound, smell, taste, or touch. For these people, the senses can be more intense or more painful or more frightening than they are for most people. People with autism often struggle to interact with others in regular ways. They may also behave, communicate, and learn in different ways than other people.

On the Spectrum

A spectrum is a range of different colors, as you might see in a rainbow. Together, the individual colors make up white light. We can think of all the people with autism as having slightly different shades of the disorder. Each has an individual set of symptoms and differences. That is why autism is more properly known as autism spectrum disorder (ASD). If you have met one person with ASD, you still have no idea what other people with ASD are actually like as individuals.

Widespread

You probably do know someone with ASD because it is relatively common. About one percent of the global population has the disorder. In the United States, one in sixty-eight children has been identified with ASD. That is equal to one person with ASD for every two classrooms of students in a school. Autism can affect anyone, regardless of their racial or social background, or where they are from. There are many reasons why people can have autism. One reason is the genes they inherit from their parents.

Statistically speaking, at least one person in this picture probably has autism. Anyone anywhere can develop this condition.

What Are the Symptoms?

People with ASD can range from being nonverbal (nonspeaking) to verbal (speaking). They can range from gifted in their abilities to severely challenged. They can range from being very sensitive to not very sensitive to touch, smells, sounds, and other sensory stimuli. Some may have normal coordination and motor skills. Others may find it difficult to walk or grasp things. However, there is a set of typical symptoms of the disorder that apply to many people with ASD. These are typical no matter where they happen to fall on the spectrum. People with autism will often:

- not make eye contact and prefer to be alone
- have unusual reactions to the way things taste, look, feel, smell, or sound
- be very interested or disinterested in people, but not know how to relate to them
- appear to not notice when people talk to them, but respond to other sounds
- have trouble understanding other people's feelings or expressions
- repeat or echo words or phrases said to them, sometimes in place of normal language
- repeat actions over and over again
- have obsessive interests
- have trouble expressing their needs using typical words or motions
- get upset by minor changes in their normal routine

Early Social Skills

Autism is a lifelong disorder, and its signs can start at as early as two years of age. This is a time when children rapidly acquire and use language, learn boundaries, and figure out how to behave in groups. Many children with ASD take longer to start talking. They also have a very hard time learning to take turns and share. They avoid pretend play, and cannot understand teasing. They may do things to stimulate their senses, such as flapping their arms, rocking to and fro, or spinning around. All of these things can make other children avoid children with ASD. This leaves these children isolated.

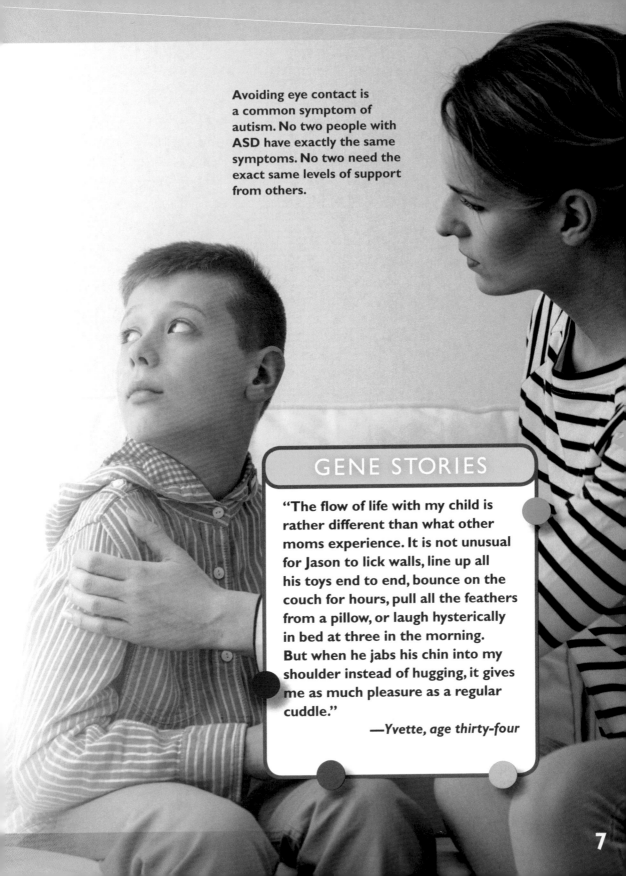

Avoiding eye contact is a common symptom of autism. No two people with ASD have exactly the same symptoms. No two need the exact same levels of support from others.

GENE STORIES

"The flow of life with my child is rather different than what other moms experience. It is not unusual for Jason to lick walls, line up all his toys end to end, bounce on the couch for hours, pull all the feathers from a pillow, or laugh hysterically in bed at three in the morning. But when he jabs his chin into my shoulder instead of hugging, it gives me as much pleasure as a regular cuddle."

—Yvette, age thirty-four

Types of Autism

All people with autism fall somewhere on the spectrum. Doctors sometimes diagnose individuals with several distinct subtypes of autism, depending on their symptoms. Today, all subtypes are technically included within ASD and are not official medical diagnoses. But, in common practice, the terms are often still used. These terms are well understood and create helpful distinctions between groups.

Common Versus Rare

Autistic disorder, or childhood autism, is the most commonly diagnosed subtype of autism. It is characterized by impaired development that becomes clear before the age of three. This typically includes abnormal social interaction and communication, and restricted repetitive behavior. Childhood disintegrative disorder, or Heller's syndrome, is the rarest and most severe subtype of autism. This condition is diagnosed when children develop normally until the age of two, then lose many of the skills they had, such as talking and walking. They may also develop certain behaviors such as repetitive mannerisms.

Unusual distress or discomfort over crowded places and loud sounds can be a sign of autism.

Asperger's Syndrome

Probably the best known subtype of autism is called Asperger's syndrome. People with this syndrome are of average or above average intelligence. They may excel at subjects ranging from art or music to math and computing. In general, they rarely have the learning disabilities that many autistic people have. Children with Asperger's do not have delayed language use. However, like other people on the spectrum, they may still have difficulties processing what others say. Many have intense, even obsessive interests from a young age. These can include interests ranging from dinosaurs and cars to reading newspapers or watching old films. These interests may change over time, or may be lifelong.

Functioning

If you are better at math than your best friend, and he or she can draw better than you can, we may simply say you have different strengths. When referring to autism spectrum disorder, these types of differences are often referred to as being higher or lower functioning. Functioning means dealing with or overcoming the challenges of everyday life. Someone who is higher functioning can speak, read, write, and interact more like people without autism. They can also handle basic life skills such as eating and getting dressed. People who are lower functioning have greater social and behavioral problems. These affect their ability to lead independent lives. These terms are widely used and generally understood. But there is no real definition to describe a person's level of functioning, based on accurate comparisons between different people with autism.

GENE STORIES

"My symptoms are in fact me, and the problem is when people want me to be someone else. The way I now explain things is that NTs (neurotypicals) see and think one way, because that's the way they are wired, and Aspies (individuals with Asperger's syndrome) see and think another way because of their wiring, too."

—Adil, age twenty

Chapter 2

Why Do People Develop Autism?

Autism is not uncommon globally, yet scientists and doctors are not entirely certain what causes it in different people. However, people with the disorder do have certain differences from the neurotypical population. These differences are evident from a physical examination of the brain.

The Brain

Your brain controls you. This pink, gray, and wrinkly organ in your skull is the headquarters of your nervous system. The nervous system is a network of nerves carrying information to and from the rest of your body. Messages flow through this network to control your senses, movement, and countless other things.

Each brain contains about 100 billion nerve cells called neurons. They are not just packed together in a big jumble. Instead, they are organized into different parts with different jobs to do. For example, the cerebellum controls coordination of movement, such as keeping balance. The limbic system is responsible for all the emotions we feel and the things we remember.

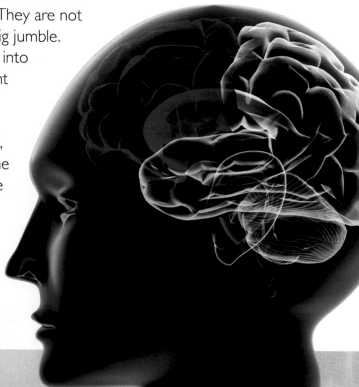

This diagram shows the close proximity of different brain parts.

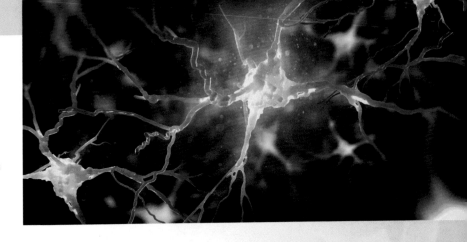

Neurons are very tiny. They connect to form vast information highways through the brain and body.

Development of the Brain

Different brain parts are in constant communication with one another, and work in a coordinated fashion. This process speeds up from birth. In a child's first few years of life, more than a million new connections form between the neurons every second. These create remarkable information highways through the brain, a bit like wires in an electrical circuit. Later, the connections are pruned to make brain circuits more efficient and faster. Different neural pathways fine-tune senses such as sight, hearing, and touch, along with motor and language skills, thinking, and memory storage.

The brain automatically puts together information to make sense of the world and to navigate it. However, in infants with autism, scientists think that there is a difference in the way brain parts communicate with one another. This makes different pathways develop, leading to different behaviors and responses to the world.

Gene Genies

In 2012, scientists carried out brain scans of people with and without autism. They discovered a significant difference in communication between brain parts. The scans showed which parts of the brain become active when people see pictures, read words, or think about certain things. In neurotypical brains, there was activity synchronization between the frontal parts and back parts. The frontal parts process what the patients see. The back parts process what images mean, and the emotions and memories they produce. In autistic brains, there was a lack of synchronization between these parts.

Among the Neurons

There are changes in communication between brain parts in people with autism. These are a result of the way neurons pass messages between each other.

Message Flow

Bundles of neurons in nerves carry many messages all the time, to and from different parts of the body. Neurons are special cells with a long part called an axon on one side. They have tufty parts called dendrites on the other side. Nerve messages move as tiny, very fast bursts of electricity through the axon of one neuron. At the end, they reach a very small gap called a synapse before the start of the dendrites of the next neuron. The messages cross over this synapse in the form of special chemicals called neurotransmitters. When enough neurotransmitters reach the next neuron, the synapse is switched on and the message is passed. Then chemicals called enzymes destroy the neurotransmitters. This clears the synapse in readiness for passing on the next message when it comes.

Not Turning Off

In people with autism, studies show that brain neurons have excess amounts of a neurotransmitter called glutamic acid. They also have lower amounts of neurotransmitters that control the amount of message flow, causing the synapses to stay activated for much longer than in people with normal neurotransmitter balance.

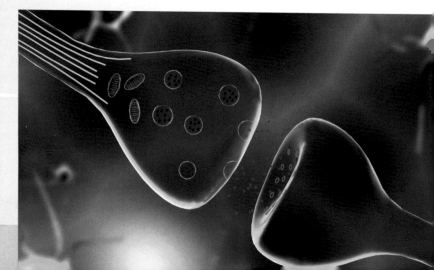

Brain function depends on neurotransmitters. These form temporary chemical bridges across nerve synapses.

Without cables and Wi-Fi, people could not tap into the wealth of stored information on computers worldwide. Now, think of how altered connections could affect function in an autistic brain.

Other neurotransmitters show changed amounts in people with autism. For example, these people typically have either too much or too little serotonin. This neurotransmitter regulates learning, memory, sense perception, and many other things. Children with autism often have high dopamine levels, too. This neurotransmitter causes the mind to race and increase sensory perception. This causes an overload on the brain's ability to process information.

Neuron Differences

Scientists have also found irregularities in the neurons of people with autism. There are sometimes too many dendrites that are spindly or highly branched. This can result in too many or too few synapses, or synapses that pass messages too strongly or too weakly. Axons can also have an abnormal structure. This leads to the disorganized passage of information through neural pathways between brain parts. These changes in wiring can have a profound effect on the way the brain works in autism.

GENE STORIES

"When your stereo is working well, the sound is sweet, crisp, and clear. But if the wiring is faulty, the sound is unpredictable. In one position it can sound great, in another the sound is muffled or weird. Sometimes you get white noise, a deafening buzz, or complete silence. Welcome to autism!"
—*Perdita, age fifteen*

Range of Causes

Scientists think that the brain and neural wiring changes associated with autism are linked to many different factors. Some of these causes are environmental and related to health conditions in individuals. Scientists are still studying to learn more about the possible causes of ASD.

Environment

When doctors refer to environment, they do not just mean whether someone lives near a park or a forest. They mean other things, such as what chemicals someone was exposed to during their childhood and what happened before or after their birth. For example, one thing that is possibly linked to an increased risk of developing autism is being born prematurely (before week thirty-five of a pregnancy). Another possible link might be being exposed to high levels of certain substances while developing in the womb. Certain environmental toxins such as pesticides, which are chemicals used to kill bugs on crops, have also been linked to ASD. Still other suspected environmental causes for ASD include a drug called sodium valproate. This is sometimes used to treat epilepsy in pregnant women.

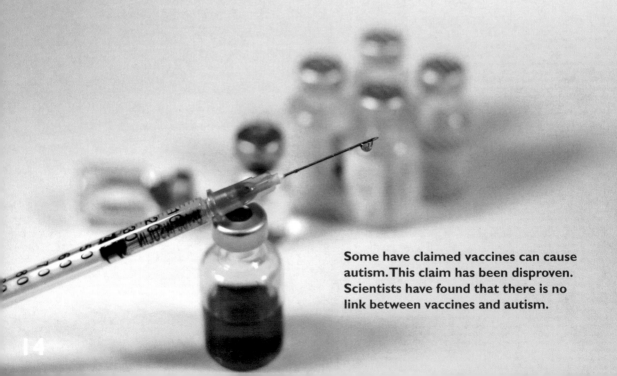

Some have claimed vaccines can cause autism. This claim has been disproven. Scientists have found that there is no link between vaccines and autism.

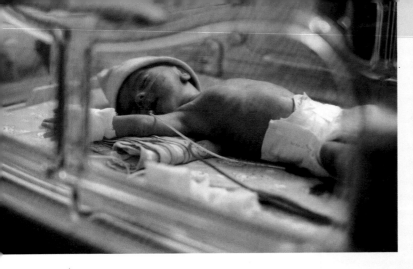

Certain conditions can have an impact on an infant's neurodevelopment. Two such conditions are premature birth and inflammatory brain infections.

Health Conditions

Several health conditions are known to be associated with the development of ASD in individuals. These include cerebral palsy, which is a neurodevelopmental disorder affecting movement and posture. It is the most common physical disability in childhood. Another is muscular dystrophy, which is a condition that gradually causes muscles to weaken. Certain viral infections such as measles and mumps can also increase the risk of ASD in children. Another possible culprit is encephalitis. This is a type of brain inflammation and swelling that is caused by cells of the immune system collecting in the brain and attacking viruses. This illness has an impact on neuron health and the abilities of synapses to transmit messages.

Things That Do Not Cause ASD

Some people have suggested that certain things cause ASD, when in reality they do not. For example, eating too much dairy or gluten, immunizations, and bad parenting do not cause ASD. In looking for evidence to prove or disprove these ideas, scientists have carried out extensive research and studies on patients. Sometimes, it is clear from the data that something is definitely not a cause. This is the case for diet, vaccines, and upbringing. Common childhood vaccines treat dangerous infectious diseases such as polio, chickenpox, measles, mumps, and rubella. Some parents thought vaccines were to blame for their children having autism. However, large-scale studies have shown that this is not true. There is no link between common childhood vaccines and ASD symptoms.

Chapter 3

Genes and Autism

Some people have diseases such as sickle cell anemia or cystic fibrosis. They inherit, or receive from their parents, genes that cause these disorders. The genes prevent cells from functioning properly in ways that lead to specific disease symptoms. In a similar manner, scientists and doctors believe that a person's genes can also influence whether that person has autism.

What Are Genes?

Genes are the blueprint of instructions found inside every cell. These instructions tell the cell how to develop, grow, and function. Cells are the building blocks of all living things. The instructions are not written down, but instead are complex structures made up of a substance called DNA. It looks kind of like a ladder twisted into a spiral. Each rung of the ladder is made from a particular sequence of chemicals, like a string of letters completing a word. These "words" tell cells what to do, just as written words in an instruction book give directions for tasks. The gene instructions involved in autism are found in every person. However, only some develop the condition. Scientists think genetic and environmental risk factors are likely what may lead to person having autism.

Set of Chromosomes

Thousands of genes are twisted and packed tightly into chromosomes inside cells. Each cell in our bodies contains twenty-three pairs of chromosomes, making forty-six altogether. When living things reproduce sexually, one chromosome of each pair from a male joins with another from a female. These produce new pairs in their offspring. Each person inherits from their parents a unique set of chromosomes with its own combination of genes. Whether a person develops a particular condition, such as autism, depends partly on the blend of genes they inherit.

Tongue rolling is one example of a trait caused by an inherited neutral gene mutation.

Mutations

Can you roll your tongue? If you can, it is because you have one version, or variant, of a gene controlling muscles in the tongue. There are different variants because of changes or mutations in the code of the DNA. Mutations can happen when DNA is not copied properly as cells divide during growth and reproduction. They can also happen when people are exposed to harmful chemicals. For example, chemicals in smoke may damage DNA and cause mutations in lung cells. Some mutations are neutral and have no effect. Some mutations are beneficial. Others can cause a disease. Scientists think that mutated genes are responsible for unusual brain development in people with autism.

Which Genes?

Scientists studying the genes of people with autism have found that, in more than 80 percent of all cases, there is no identifiable genetic cause. However, the remaining 20 percent of people have autistic symptoms resulting from neurological conditions. These conditions are caused by a mutation in a single gene or chromosome region.

Gene mutations contribute to ASD. These found on several of the normal set of fort human chromosomes.

Studies with Mice

Scientists study single-gene disorders using mice in laboratories. They use special techniques to mutate or even to remove the normal copy of the gene so the mice mimic the human disorder. They then examine how the genes work in their normal and mutated forms. Scientists have concluded that genes act similar to control knobs. They regulate the complex neural pathways in the brain, such as by changing the quality and quantity of synapses. They have discovered a handful of genes that are reliably linked to the symptoms of autism.

Tuberous sclerosis complex (TSC): TSC is caused by a gene mutation on chromosome 9 or 16. This results in benign (noncancerous) tumors in the brain, skin, and internal organs. These can cause anything from skin problems to physical and learning disabilities. Studies report that up to 60 percent of people with TSC show ASD-like characteristics. These include poor social interaction, absent or abnormal speech, and repeated behaviors.

Cornelia de Lange syndrome (CdLS): CdLS is caused mostly by a gene deletion on chromosome 5. Symptoms that would normally indicate ASD are found in 50 to 65 percent of people with CdLS. Social anxiety, shyness, and refusal to speak except in certain environments or to certain people are common in people with CdLS.

Fragile X syndrome (FXS):
This is the most common cause of inherited learning disability. It results from an excess of genetic code forming a fragile site on the X chromosome. Symptoms of FXS are similar to CdLS. Around one-third of individuals with the syndrome have symptoms typical of autism spectrum disorder.

There are other conditions or disorders in which people have fewer symptoms that overlap with autism. They include Angelman, Rett, and Down syndromes. Unlike those with autism, people with Down syndrome are usually skilled at social interaction and have good language skills.

Gene Genies

Scientists have identified a gene called **FMR1** which, when mutated, causes **FXS**. The mutation makes too little FMRP, a protein that restricts the manufacture of many proteins at synapses. In its absence, dendrites on neurons grow wildly and with more spines. However, the spines are longer and thinner than normal, so their synapse strength and communication abilities are reduced.

People with Down syndrome have an extra copy of chromosome 21. This causes developmental changes leading to physical and mental disabilities.

In the Family

The study of single-gene disorders provides one strand of evidence for genes playing a role in autism. So does the study of the spread of autism through the population, which shows patterns of inheritance in families.

Patterns

Scientists and doctors called epidemiologists study populations of people. They examine medical records to find patterns of illness. They focus on patterns of illness in families to estimate their heritability. This is the likelihood that something is due to genes. For example, one family member has an illness. There is a higher incidence of that same disease in that family than there is in the general population. That means it is likely that genes play a significant role in the spread of the condition.

There are several patterns that support this theory. Epidemiologists have found that males are four times more likely than females to develop autism. This is possibly because males have just one X chromosome, while females have two. So, males may be more sensitive to gene mutations on that chromosome. Also, if one sibling is autistic, then another sibling has a 4 percent greater risk of developing the disorder than someone without an autistic sibling. For a brother of a male with autism, the risk is around four times what it is for a sister. Siblings of someone with autism also have a higher-than-average risk of developing other mental health disorders. These disorders include attention deficit hyperactivity disorder (ADHD).

ASD can run in the family. If one sibling has it, another sibling has a higher-than-average chance of developing the disorder.

Twins

Studies of twins are important to epidemiologists. Identical twins share all of their genes, whereas non-identical twins share only half. As a result, identical twins are more likely to share genetically based conditions. Scientists report that if one identical twin has autism, the other twin has around a 90 percent chance of developing the condition. This is nine times the heritability than that reported for non-identical twins.

Identical twins inherit exactly the same genes. If one twin has ASD, it is very likely the other twin does, too.

Gene Genies

In 2014, researchers in the United States examined the genes and chromosomes of around 750 children with autism. They found that the girls had larger mutation regions on their chromosomes. They also had a greater proportion of severe mutations that affect protein production and cause neurodevelopmental problems than boys had. It seems that it takes more mutations to trigger autism in girls than it does in boys. Data also revealed that women may pass on gene mutations involved in autism, but, they appear to be better protected than men from getting the disorder.

Chapter 4

Diagnosing and Treating Autism

When a sick patient goes to a clinic, the patient's doctor or other health care workers will carry out tests. These include analyzing blood samples to find out what is wrong. Such tests help doctors diagnose anything from heart disease to a bacterial infection. They also help them to determine what treatment a patient needs to feel better. However, there are no simple medical tests for diagnosing ASD. Screening for ASD is a longer, more involved process.

Developmental Screening

Developmental screening is a short test to tell if children are learning basic skills by the right age. The doctor asks the parents questions about

Developmental screening is a normal and important assessment of early health, skills, and behavior.

what a child has been like since birth. They talk and play with the child during an exam to see how the child speaks, behaves, learns, and moves. A delay in normal development in any of those areas, such as not responding to his or her name or copying phrases, could be one sign of ASD.

Autism does not reveal itself the same way in all children. Studies have shown that one-third to one-half of all parents of children with ASD noticed a problem before their child's first birthday. Nearly 80 to 90 percent saw problems by twenty-four months of age. To spot and track developmental changes through time, it is important that parents take their children for screening at regular intervals. Screenings are recommended at nine, eighteen, and twenty-four or thirty months of age.

The Full Picture

A screening session is brief. Whatever a doctor finds, there is still the possibility that the child was having a bad or unusual day. It may not be representative of the child's actual mental state, abilities, or behaviors. That is why developmental history and input are important in reaching an accurate diagnosis. These can come from family members, caregivers, as well as teachers or workers at schools, colleges, or childcare centers. The process of diagnosis can also rule out other conditions, such as Down syndrome and Tourette syndrome. These conditions could produce similar symptoms to autism.

Gene Genies

In 2017, scientists in the United States developed a medical test that could be used in the future to help diagnose autism. Autistic and non-autistic people were asked to focus on a moving target on a screen. Scientists filmed and analyzed eye movements. They found that the eyes of autistic people missed or overshot the target more often than the eyes of non-autistic people. It is likely that this indicates a difference in neurodevelopment of the cerebellum. This brain part controls muscle movement, balance, and speech. It also controls emotion, learning, and understanding.

Diagnostic Evaluation

Screening is the first step toward an autism diagnosis. When someone is screened and suspected of having the disorder, they may be given a more thorough diagnostic evaluation. It is important to be certain of such a diagnosis because it has big implications for a patient. It can help explain to them and to others the difficulties they have had in life. It may also enable them to get better access to support that can help them in the future.

People suspected of having autism go through a diagnostic evaluation. A hearing test is included.

Comprehensive Review

A diagnostic evaluation includes a thorough assessment of behavior and development. It also includes a number of tests. For example, people have hearing tests to see how sensitive they are to noises. They can also show whether deafness is preventing them from hearing what others say and responding to it. They also have eye tests, gene testing to screen for genetic disorders, and other medical tests. The evaluation is often carried out by specialist doctors. These include developmental pediatricians, who are doctors with special training in child development and children with special needs. They also include child psychiatrists, who are doctors specializing in diagnosing and treating mental illnesses in children.

Standard Tests

Although autism takes many forms, its diagnosis must be unbiased. That is why specialists use standard tests to assess patients for ASD. They use the *Diagnostic and Statistical Manual*, also called DSM-5. In DSM-5, people are defined as autistic if they satisfy certain criteria. These include having major difficulty in communicating and interacting with people in many situations. Experts need to know how severe a patient's ASD symptoms are to decide how much support they need. For example, someone with Level 3 ASD has very severe problems communicating. They also have such difficulty coping with change that they will need a great deal of support.

GENE STORIES

"My parents gently broke the news to me that I had autism, and helped me to explore my strengths and differences. This helped me to learn how to adapt and survive in this world. It makes me so sad to hear about kids who only found out about their diagnosis when they read the word 'autistic' next to their name on a classroom list, or who thought their problems making friends as a teenager were a result of being ugly rather than a medical condition."

—*Darius, age eighteen*

Learning How to Behave and Communicate

The earlier someone is diagnosed with autism, the better. This will give the person more time to learn how to behave and communicate. They can then become better at dealing with any difficulties they have. They can also make the most of the things they are good at.

Behavior

For people with ASD, it can take a lot of effort to behave the way other people expect them to. Learning these skills may require special teachers who are experts in helping people with special needs. These professionals encourage and reward positive behaviors, such as helping others. They ignore or gently discourage negative behaviors, such as shouting out loud. They also know how to maximize a child's abilities. For example, many autistic children have short attention spans. They respond best if tests always happen the same way, following a script. Knowing this, teachers may break down skills into smaller, easier steps.

People diagnosed with ASD may also have help from occupational therapists. These professionals help people with autism to live as independently as possible. They teach them life skills, such as how to

Expert help from teachers can transform how someone with ASD understands and expresses emotions.

dress and feed themselves. Even bathing can be a challenge. People with autism may need help learning that water can drown and hot water can burn. They may need to overcome difficulties with the feel of water on their skin.

Communication

Treatment of autism involves helping people communicate better. Speech therapists teach patients to speak more clearly and build up a better vocabulary. They can teach them to speak in varied tones, stop repeating what people say, listen better, and wait for gaps in a conversation before they speak. People with autism must also learn not to take the meaning of phrases literally. For example, "It's raining cats and dogs" refers to the weather, not to animals falling from the sky! Speech therapists may help nonverbal patients use pictures or gestures to communicate, too.

Communicating with others comes naturally to most people. But people with ASD may need help to learn this behavior.

GENE STORIES

"My daughter Irene used to run off into the street. She couldn't understand that her own behavior could lead to problems. She also struggled to understand people's facial expressions. To help her, I learned how to draw pictures and comic strips showing different situations and what different emotions look like on faces. Looking at the pictures has helped her to understand what's dangerous and what's acceptable, and to read people better. It has helped Irene enormously."

—Mark, age forty-four

Medication and Other Treatments

People with a simple headache often take headache pills to get rid of the pain. People with autism do not have such an easy solution. There is no single medication to treat the range of symptoms associated with ASD. There is no treatment that is specific to autism. Different medications can ease particularly serious impacts of autism in some people. But they should be seen as only one part of an important range of therapies. These include psychological, behavioral, and educational programs.

Aggressive and challenging behavior: Tantrums, self-harm, and other negative behaviors may be calmed with a class of drugs called antipsychotics. For example, risperidone changes the amount and action of certain neurotransmitters in brain synapses. These neurotransmitters include serotonin and dopamine.

Depression: Continuous low mood can be treated with antidepressants. These medications flood the brain with neurotransmitters that improve communication between neurons. They also strengthen information pathways in brain parts controlling mood.

Any of these medications, plus medications to treat seizures, sleep problems, and other autistic symptoms, can have side effects. Side effects are secondary, usually unwelcome, responses to taking a drug. They may include weight gain, drowsiness, or rashes. To reduce the risk of these side effects, the amount and frequency of autism-related medications needs to be carefully monitored by a doctor. Regular check-ups are needed to see how the medication is working.

Other Treatments

Here are just a few of the many other possible therapies that can help people diagnosed with ASD.

Talk therapy: Many people with ASD can benefit from talk therapy sessions with trained psychologists. These professionals can help people identify unhealthy thoughts and behaviors in themselves and others. They can replace them with healthy, positive ones. The aim of talk therapy is to help people understand how their thoughts, behaviors, and emotions interact with and affect one another.

Sensory interventions: Some people with autism may have highly acute senses that can be helped by specialist interventions. For example, aromatherapy can help people overcome aversion to particular smells. Auditory treatment can help people retrain their ears to block out unnecessary background noise so they can concentrate on speech.

Music therapy: Singing songs can help people with autism learn and understand language, link words together, and learn when not to make sounds. Making music on a variety of instruments helps with motor skills and nonverbal self-expression, too.

Animal therapy: Horseback riding, working with dogs, or swimming with dolphins can all soothe sensory stimulation. They can help some people with autism learn about behavior and communication.

Animal therapy includes petting and being in close contact with animals. It can help people with ASD to control their sensory overloads.

Chapter 5
Living with Autism

We are all individuals with quirks, strengths, and weaknesses. So it is no surprise that autism is not a one-size-fits-all disorder. People with autism and those who support them need varying strategies. These help them cope in our ever-changing world.

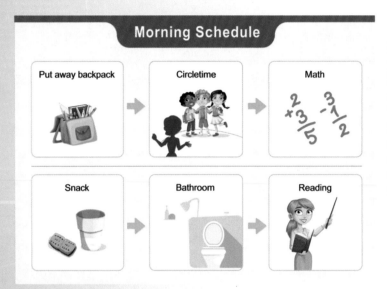

Pictorial schedules can be helpful and comforting. They can be an important source of support to people with **ASD.**

SPELL It Out

One strategy is based around five principles that start with the letters S-P-E-L-L.

Structure: People with ASD often feel safer, less anxious, and learn best if their lives have structure. Predictable environments and routines help them rely on others less. They also help them to independently go about their lives. Something that provides structure is visual aids such as objects, photos, pictures, or cartoon strips. These help people with autism understand things in ways that written words cannot. They can be about anything from the proper use of toilets to what to expect when going to the movies.

Positive: Positive approaches and expectations help people with autism build self-confidence and self-esteem. For example, someone may have trouble coping in social situations but they have helpers who have positive expectations. If these helpers really believe the person with autism can succeed in social events, that person will probably make a greater effort. Afterward, the person may feel glad to have participated. They may also be motivated to learn better social skills or ways to make social situations less stressful.

Empathy: It is important for people with autism to try to explain to others how they see the world. Others must also learn how to see the world from the autistic person's standpoint. Empathy allows people to see what motivates or interests people with autism. It helps them understand what preoccupies or frightens them.

Low arousal: People with autism may be unpleasantly aroused by particular sensory stimuli. So, it is helpful if they live, study, and work in uncluttered places. Triggers such as noise levels and color schemes should be carefully considered. Also, consider a quieter restaurant with fewer, clear choices of what to order. This may suit a person with ASD better than a noisy, busy place with a long, hard-to-understand menu.

Links: Someone with autism may seem trapped inside his or her own experience. However, they really benefit from strong links with others. An autistic person may prefer working with a regular caregiver or therapist. This is better than seeing a different person each time.

People with autism often prefer structured days with fixed sequences of tasks. These can be shown on checklists or large-scale visual calendars.

People with ASD need a trusted, supportive network of family and friends. This allows them to forge strong and important links with others.

Family Life

Imagine what shopping in a supermarket is like for a person with autism. If aisles have been rearranged, the person may get anxious and start shouting and flailing his or her arms. The change may make it hard for them to find a favorite food. They may get upset if getting there was made tricky by construction or a traffic jam. Now think of how the stares and remarks of others could make the situation worse.

This is just one of the many day-to-day situations that can be incredibly stressful. This is not only for a person with autism, but also for the family members who are with that person. Autism in a family can have many impacts on different family members.

Family dynamics can become difficult when one family member is autistic. Good communication helps to keep things positive.

Parents or main caregivers:
These people are responsible for dealing with difficult behaviors, organizing treatments for symptoms, and helping to organize routines for the person with ASD. They have the worries of planning for the future work, study, or independent living of the person. All of this occurs alongside regular tasks from their own work. This includes preparing meals, and looking after other children and older relatives.

Siblings: Siblings of someone with autism can understandably feel overlooked by parents at home. They may feel very embarrassed by their autistic sibling's behavior in public. It can feel unfair if the autistic person is not scolded for what they do, but the neurotypical sibling is.

GENE STORIES

"My parents tried to make time for me, but they were often too stressed and focused on my brother Rory to listen to me. I would lock myself in my room and cry, while my brother watched *The Lion King* for the millionth time, shouting downstairs. Doors, windows, and cupboards had to be locked to stop Rory from harming himself. And I couldn't leave out any school work because he might ruin it."

—*Brooke, age nineteen*

Helping Family Life

Autism affects a whole family. It is important for people to discuss with each other their feelings about it. This can sometimes be easier when families get the help of a trained family therapist. It is also very helpful for families to stay involved in their community. They can participate in everything from fundraising events to walking in the local park, and not shut themselves away. Staying involved allows the person with autism to experience different social settings and relationships. Some families meet up with other families with autistic members to share experiences with empathetic people.

Changing Special Needs

People with ASD often have special needs through life. They may require different levels of assistance or support to help them achieve their potential and cope with demands and challenges.

At School and College

Many children with ASD go to regular schools. Some, such as those with Asperger's syndrome, may be happy without extra help. They may excel at the top of the class in particular subjects, such as math and computers. However, they may need help engaging in topics that may not be of great interest to them, such as literature or foreign languages. Some people with autism may need help mixing with other children at recess. They may benefit from an older "buddy" who hangs out with them in the schoolyard. A buddy can help them understand the rules of games, and make sure they do not get bullied. Other young people with autism may benefit from attending special schools. There, they can learn and socialize in a more individually structured, less pressured environment. Everyone is different, so what may help one person is not the same as what may help another person.

Young people with Asperger's syndrome sometimes have abilities beyond those expected for their age group.

Becoming an Adult

People with greater difficulties from autism may need continued high levels of support into adulthood. They may leave home and live in a place where resident assistants and other personnel can watch over them. Support workers may help them find job opportunities. They may find work in which the environment or task expectations do not cause excessive anxiety.

Although the challenges can be considerable, many people with autism go on to live independently. They work regular jobs, often excelling in their fields, and thrive into older age.

However, it is an unfortunate fact that many people with autism struggle. They may not have much money because they have trouble getting or holding good jobs. They may find it difficult to make and keep friends or attend social events. Some people with ASD develop mental health conditions such as depression. This may be caused by years of isolation, loneliness, and side effects from medications to treat symptoms.

Some individuals with autism are extraordinarily creative compared to their peers.

GENE STORIES

"My Asperger's daughter attended public school until age twelve, but she was just a drop in the bucket there. No one paid any attention to her needs or tried to help her. We finally withdrew her and placed her in a school for special-needs students. It was a hard decision to make, but we have been ecstatic with the results. With the right atmosphere and emotional support, our daughter is now exceling academically and is on a college track. Many challenges lie ahead, but at least now she has a chance."

—Chris, age fifty

Chapter 6
Autism and Gene Therapy

In the future, people with ASD may be able to lessen their symptoms. They may even alter their neurodevelopment by altering the genes responsible for the disorder. This is possible because scientists have found ways to swap out mutations that cause illnesses. They then replace them with healthy versions. This process is called gene therapy.

Altering Genes

Gene therapy targets particular genes in a living thing. Scientists first identify a mutated section of DNA on a gene that is not functioning properly. The gene might be causing a health problem. They then replace the faulty gene with a new, functioning gene. The technique of editing or making changes to genes was first developed in the 1970s. However, it is only in recent times that improved equipment has been available for scientists to use. These include powerful computers and better laboratory techniques for gene editing. Gene therapy is not yet in use to treat autism. However, it has already been successful in treating some illnesses. For example, it can shrivel and shrink some skin cancer tumors.

Many Genes

Scientists have so far identified more than 21,000 genes in every human. Each gene is in a different location on one of the twenty-three chromosomes. Each gene has a different job to do for our bodies. For example, specific genes may cause cells to make particular proteins to build and repair themselves. Or they may regulate the way sets of cells work together. Many gene functions have been discovered. Some conditions involve just one gene function. Others, including ASD, are polygenic. This means they involve many genes, and are controlled by their complex and subtle interaction.

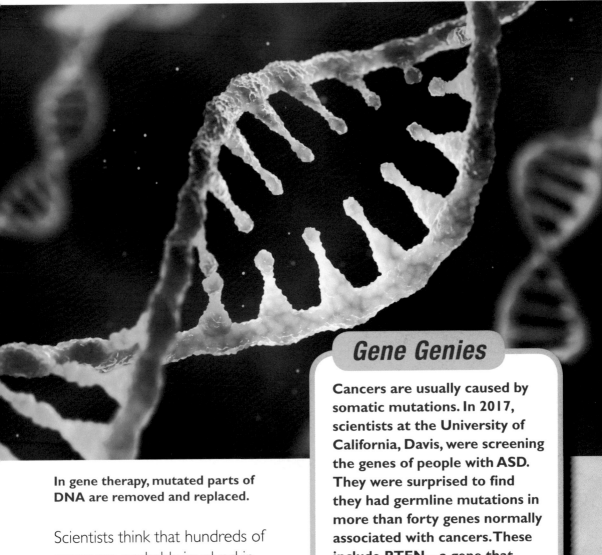

In gene therapy, mutated parts of **DNA** are removed and replaced.

Scientists think that hundreds of genes are probably involved in autism. They think that people are born with most mutations of these genes, which they carry in nearly every cell. These are called germline mutations. Mutations that occur after birth, affecting a smaller set of the body's cells, are called somatic mutations.

Gene Genies

Cancers are usually caused by somatic mutations. In 2017, scientists at the University of California, Davis, were screening the genes of people with ASD. They were surprised to find they had germline mutations in more than forty genes normally associated with cancers. These include PTEN—a gene that normally controls cell growth. When mutated, it can cause overgrowth of neurons during neurodevelopment. Later in life, it can also cause growth in cell size and number, leading to cancers.

Viruses have knobs on the outside. These lock onto the surfaces of the cells they target.

Gene Therapy Method

Gene therapy uses a person's own cells to treat that person. It employs unique cells called stem cells. Unlike most body cells, which do specialized jobs, stem cells are unspecialized at first. But they can turn into specialized cells as needed. They can also divide over and over. Scientists can get stem cells from different places around the body, such as the umbilical cord and the skin.

Gene Transporters

In laboratories, scientists use viruses to introduce particular genes into stem cells. If you have ever had a cold, then you have been attacked by a virus. Viruses are incredibly small living things, much smaller than bacteria. They have a small amount of DNA in genes protected inside a protein layer. They can only reproduce and increase in number once they get inside other living cells. There, they use energy from the host cell to start making copies of their genetic material. Scientists modify viruses to transport DNA. They first remove any of the virus's own genes that cause sicknesses in people. They then replace them with the normal functioning gene. This gene is added in the gene therapy procedure.

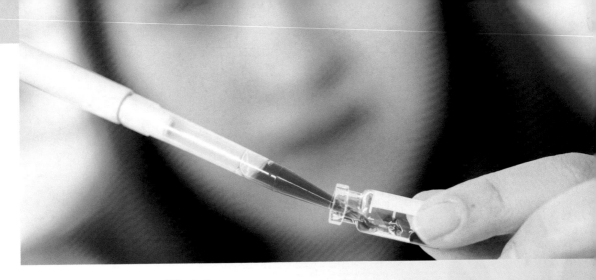

Lab workers create modified viruses. They also create large numbers of stem cells for them to "infect."

Next Step

Scientists add a solution containing the modified viruses. It also contains chemicals to help the stem cells divide more quickly. The solution is then washed off. Scientists inject the stem cells "infected" with the normal gene into the person receiving gene therapy. Once inside the body, the stem cells specialize. The normal copies of the genes start to do their work. In gene therapy for autism, stem cells could form neurons in the brain that make the correct proteins. They may also regulate normal growth and function of dendrites and synapses. This may mend and regrow some neural pathways, increasing communication between brain parts.

Gene Genies

In 2017, twenty-five children aged two to six with ASD took part in a new stem cell treatment at Duke University in North Carolina. Each child was given a transfusion of one to two billion blood stem cells taken from their own umbilical cord. This was donated at birth and frozen. Around 70 percent showed improvements. They had better vocabulary and speech, and fewer repetitive behaviors. They had better play and social interaction. Doctors are cautiously optimistic that immune cells in the cord blood moved into the brain. They think the cells changed brain connections and stopped neuron inflammation, reducing autism symptoms.

The Challenges of Gene Therapy

Gene therapy for autism is promising. However, it is a more challenging and controversial therapy than others. The techniques can work well in an artificial laboratory setting. But they are more difficult to predict in the real world—in real patients.

Beating the Shield

The body's defensive shield, the immune system, is populated by a mobile army of white blood cells. These cells defend the body's cells when they detect attack by other organisms, such as viruses. Some seek out and destroy the viruses. Others create proteins to recognize the attackers to speed up defenses on future attacks. The viruses used in gene therapy can be recognized as intruders, too. The immune system can go into attack mode as the result of gene therapy. If this happens, the body uses up lots of energy and the patient feels exhausted. An immune attack can also cause tissue inflammation and even failure of organs such as the liver. Scientists are working hard to find viruses that are less likely to trigger an immune response.

Scientists have tested gene therapy techniques for autism on laboratory mice.

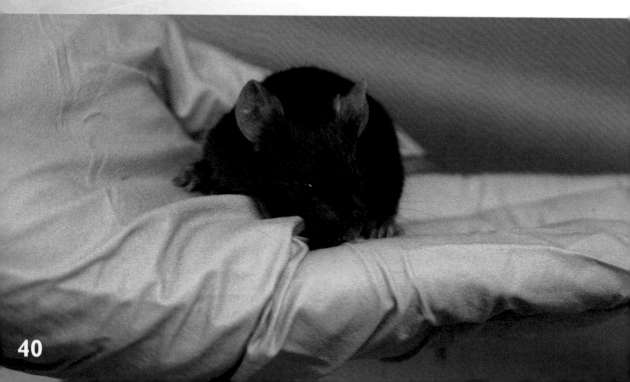

Sensitive Tissue

Many normal medicines can be injected into the blood. The body circulates the medicine and the blood around the body to where they are useful. But there is a barrier between blood and brain that gene therapy transporters, such as viruses, cannot pass. To get edited cells into the sensitive brain tissue that controls autism, doctors must inject them with a needle. This is potentially harmful because the needle could cause physical damage to the brain. That, in turn, could affect the way a patient experiences moods, thoughts, memories, and other aspects of the brain's function.

Injections for gene therapy of autism will only work if they can hit their targets accurately.

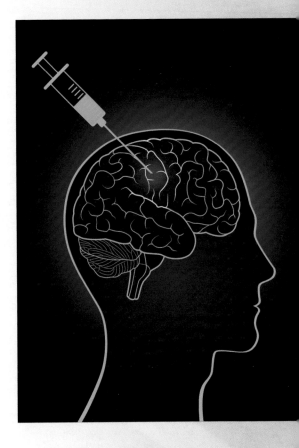

Gene Genies

Around 1 percent of people with autism lack a working copy of the SHANK3 gene. This gene is critical for brain development. It contains instructions for a protein that helps neurons communicate with one another. It also helps organize many other brain proteins in coordinating neuronal responses to incoming nerve messages. Researchers bred mice with autistic symptoms by using laboratory techniques to turn off SHANK3. The symptoms include repetitive behavior such as constant grooming and social avoidance. They then turned the gene back on by giving the mice a special drug. The autism symptoms reversed, even in adult mice. This finding hints that brains in mature mice can at least partially rewire themselves. This work is exciting. But lengthy trials must be carried out to make sure the technique is safe before it can be tested on humans.

Autism Improvements

Gene therapy is highly promising. It has the potential for rapid improvement in symptoms of autism, even rewiring brains. But, at this time, there is great uncertainty about what improvements are possible or desirable.

Realistic Hope?

Stem cell therapy is increasingly being offered commercially. Centers promise major transformations—at a cost—for people with a variety of conditions. Desperate parents and caregivers of people with ASD may be tempted to try anything to help, even if it nearly bankrupts them. However, research is still being worked on, and very few therapies that are currently available have been proven to be completely safe and effective.

The way forward is for reputable organizations to carry out more research into the effectiveness of treatments at these centers. The public needs to know what improvements or changes they can realistically expect from such treatments. A quick or easy treatment for ASD does not exist. Today, in practice, it usually takes a lot of love, time, work, and perseverance to help people with autism.

Which Changes?

Gene therapy is controversial for several reasons. One is that it opens the possibility for misuse. Autism is a condition that is seen by some as bad for an individual. For this reason, some people might want to remove from cells the mutated genes that are responsible for the disorder. However, who decides what is normal and abnormal in a person's set of genes? Could the use of gene therapy make society less tolerant of people who are different, and who have different abilities? Could it also remove the vital variety in the ways people think that drives societies?

Getting Personal

Every person with ASD has a different set of symptoms and reactions to various therapies. For this reason, scientists are developing personalized gene therapy to help symptoms. Neurons grown from a patient's own stem cells could be tested in laboratories by turning genes off and on. Then scientists may be able to figure out how genes work together to control what goes on in a person's brain. They can then develop specific therapies. These may include more effective drugs to calm anxiety or to strengthen synapses and brain communication.

Alternative brain wiring has driven great creativity in humans. Examples range from NASA space programs to the creation of music to scientific theorems such as those of Einstein.

A greater understanding and celebration of diversity in society can help people with ASD.

Hope for the Future

Today, autism is on the rise and people are not really sure why. Part of the reason might be better screening. But part may be some as-yet-unknown combination of genetic and environmental influences. The wider public is becoming aware that ASD is the result of physical differences in brain wiring. It is a health condition as real as cancer, not a sign of weakness or poor behavior. However, society needs to develop a better understanding of people with autism. We need to make provisions for them and the diversity of their neurodevelopment.

Lifelong support and understanding can help people with ASD reach their full potential. Future treatments being developed may also help.

Gene Genies

The Autism Speaks **MSSNG** Project is the world's largest genetic screening program for autism. Its name represents the missing information about autism that scientists are seeking. So far, they have analyzed genes in more than 5,000 families affected by autism. They found sixty-one gene variations in common—most controlling the production of proteins and other chemicals in brains. Researchers say that some of the same gene variants may be found in people with autism at different ends of the spectrum. Some individuals who carry the mutations are not autistic. Studies of these genes will help scientists determine how they might adjust future therapies for symptom severity. They have also found that genetic differences are not just "spelling mistakes" of codes making up gene **DNA**. They may also consist of repeated or deleted sequences and chromosome abnormalities. Thanks to collaboration with Google Cloud, this vast amount of information will be made accessible to researchers everywhere at no cost.

GENE STORIES

"Don't ask *if* your child with autism can do something—ask *how* he or she can do it. Find the right support or skill that will span the gap to that goal. Some goals seem impossible, but the child who grows up asking 'How can I?' learns to see challenges as a chance for creativity and maybe even growth."

—*Latha, age forty-eight*

Changing Therapies

It is clear that with education, social support, medication, and patience, many people with autism can have full and rewarding lives. Effectiveness of therapies is being improved by earlier screening. For example, some new types of brain scans can spot brain disconnects in children as young as six months of age. And new therapies are emerging all the time to treat ASD symptoms. These are helped by projects for screening mutated genes and determining their functions and interactions in more families with ASD.

Glossary

cancer A disease caused by abnormalities in body cells.

chromosomes Parts of a cell that contain the genes that control how we grow and what we become.

complex Consisting of many different and connected parts.

dendrites Short projections from the central part of a neuron that end in synapses.

diagnose Identify an illness or condition.

DNA Short for deoxyribonucleic acid, DNA contains the instructions an organism needs to develop, live, and reproduce.

environmental Relating to someone's surroundings and other external factors.

epidemiologists Doctors who deal with the incidence and frequency of diseases.

genes Parts of cells that control or influence the way a person looks, grows, and develops.

heritability The measure of a trait's tendency to be inherited.

immune system Body parts that work together to protect the body against disease.

inflammation Swelling and redness due to immune activity.

mimic To act or behave similar to something else.

mutations Significant changes in the structure and usual function of genes.

nervous system The network of nerve cells and fibers that transmits nerve impulses between parts of the body.

neural pathways Lines of communication between different brain parts via neurons.

neurodevelopmental Related to the brain's neuron development, influencing performance or functioning.

neurons Nerve fibers that carry messages between the brain and the rest of the body.

neurotransmitters Substances that transmit messages between neurons.

neurotypicals People whose brains function in a typical way.

occupational therapists Health professionals who help people overcome barriers preventing them from doing activities independently.

pediatricians Doctors specializing in childhood disease and development

psychiatrists Doctors who diagnose and treat mental illnesses.

screening Process of identifying the possible presence or risk of a health condition.

self-esteem Confidence in one's own worth or abilities.

side effects Unwanted effects of drugs, chemicals, or other medical treatment.

special needs Physical, emotional, or behavioral difficulties causing individuals to need special assistance.

speech therapists Health workers who treat and support people with verbal communication difficulties.

stem cells Cells that can divide over and over to produce not only more stem cells, but also cells that can turn into many different types of cell.

stimuli Things that cause responses, such as a loud bang causing someone to startle.

symptoms Changes in the body or mind caused by a disease or health condition.

synapse Gap over which neurons pass messages.

synchronization Operation or activity of two or more things at the same time or rate.

therapies Treatments intended to relieve or heal a disorder.

threshold A point that must be passed for something to occur.

toxins Poisons.

transfusion Transfer of blood into a person.

triggers Things that make something happen by a particular action, process, or situation.

umbilical cord The part linking a developing baby with its mother's womb.

viruses Tiny organisms that invade and live in body cells and cause disease.

Wi-Fi A facility that allows computers, smartphones, and other devices to connect to the Internet and to communicate with each other wirelessly in a specific area.

For Further Reading

Higashida, Naoki. *The Reason I Jump: The Inner Voice of a Thirteen-Year-Old Boy with Autism.* New York, NY: Random House, 2016.

Kraus, J. D. *The Aspie Teen's Survival Guide: Candid Advice for Teens, Tweens, and Parents, from a Young Man with Asperger's Syndrome.* Arlington, TX: Future Horizons, 2010.

McHenry, Irene, and Carol Moog. *The Autism Playbook for Teens: Imagination-Based Mindfulness Activities to Calm Yourself, Build Independence & Connect with Others.* Oakland, CA: Instant Help Books, 2014.

Peete, Holly Robinson, Ryan Elizabeth Peete, and R.J. Peete. *Same But Different: Teen Life on the Autism Express.* New York, NY: Scholastic Press, 2016.

Poole, H.W. *Autism Spectrum Disorders.* Broomall, PA: Mason Crest, 2016.

Students of Limpsfield Grange School and Vicky Martin. *M Is for Autism.* Philadelphia, PA: Jessica Kingsley Publishers, 2015.

Tabone, Francis. *Autism Spectrum Disorder: The Ultimate Teen Guide.* Lanham, MD: Rowman & Littlefield, 2016.

Verdick, Elizabeth, and Elizabeth Reeve. *The Survival Guide for Kids with Autism Spectrum Disorders (And Their Parents).* Minneapolis, MN: Free Spirit Publishing, 2012.

Index